Amazing
AEROPLANES

Tony Mitton and
Ant Parker

KINGFISHER

Whoosh

An aeroplane's amazing,
for it travels through the sky,

above the clouds, for miles and miles,
so very fast and high!

An airport is the place you go
to take a trip by air.

You check in at the terminal to show
you've paid your fare.

The ground crew weigh your baggage
and load it in the hold.

And then you take the walkway to the plane,
when you are told.

The flight deck's where the captain
and co-pilot do their jobs.
They both know how to fly the plane
with all its dials and knobs.

They radio Control Tower to check
the runway's clear.
They can't take off unless it is,
with other planes so near.

By intercom, the captain on the flight deck
says hello.

You have to do your seat belt up,
before the plane can go!

A plane is big and heavy,
yet it climbs up really high.

It zooms along the runway
and soars into the sky.

Its wings hold big jet engines,
which are loud and very strong.
They suck in air and blow it through
to whoosh the plane along.

When the plane moves fast enough,
the air around's so swift
it pushes up beneath the wings
and makes the whole plane lift.

Soon the plane is in the air,
so now you're on your flight.
The cabin crew look after you
and see that you're all right.

They bring you drinks and magazines
and trays of food to eat.
And sometimes there's a film to watch
while sitting in your seat.

When the journey's over,
the captain lands the plane.
Control Tower have to say it's safe
for coming down again.

You sit with seat belt fastened,
there's a bumpy, rumbling sound –
the wheels are making contact
and the plane is on the ground!

At last the doors are opening.
Then out you come with smiles.

So give a cheer! For look, you're here.
You've flown for miles and miles.

Aeroplane bits

control tower
from here the air traffic controllers direct the planes and tell pilots when to take off and land safely

flight deck
sometimes called the **cockpit**, this is where the pilot and co-pilot sit

wheel
the wheels fold away while the plane is in the air

hold
this is the space where heavy luggage is stored

wing
the wings are hollow to make them as light as possible and a smooth shape so they move through the air easily

jet engine
jet engines blow out air and gas to push the plane forward — the gas is made by burning fuel

terminal
this is the building at the airport where passengers go to catch a plane

TERMINAL

One day, a tall Green PaintBear named Gregory Green was moving into a new house on the other side of town, the purple side.

All the PaintBears on the purple side of town heard the news! Finally, someone was moving into the empty house on their block. They watched the movers carry things into the house all day and late into the night.

But the next morning, to their great surprise, they saw a Green PaintBear standing in the yard. What a shock! A Green PaintBear in their neighborhood?

Purple PaintBears always believed that Green PaintBears were mean.
Rumors they heard about them over the years made them believe this;
even though no one in the neighborhood ever met one.

Believing these rumors, all the Purple PaintBears dared not to speak with Gregory Green. Gregory became very sad.

One day, a Purple PaintBear named Pauly Purple started to think, *Maybe the rumors are not true.*

Pauly Purple never saw Gregory Green acting mean and neither did any of his Purple PaintBear friends.

Pauly Purple thought, *How would I feel? What if I was the only Purple PaintBear living on the green side of town? What if no one talked or played with me?*

The more Pauly Purple thought about it, the sadder he became. He wondered, *What if Gregory Green is sad and lonely because we are all staying away from him?*

Suddenly, Pauly Purple had a great idea. "What if I go over to Gregory Green's house with a plate full of cookies? Then I will see for myself if he really is mean." As Pauly Purple stood on the porch, he nervously rang Gregory Green's doorbell.

Quickly, the door opened! Gregory Green appeared. Instead of a frown, he had a bright, friendly smile. And in a happily surprised voice, he said, "Come in! Come in!" Pauly Purple went inside, and they talked and talked and talked. They found out that they had a lot in common as they ate all the cookies.

They discovered they both liked to laugh, play games, and eat homemade chocolate chip cookies.

As Pauly Purple walked home, he learned how ridiculous he and the other Purple PaintBears were to believe those rumors.

The next day, Pauly Purple told all the other Purple PaintBears about his wonderful day with Gregory Green. He explained, "The rumors about Green PaintBears are not true. Gregory is just like you and me!"

Sadly, the Purple PaintBears did not believed him. Pauly Purple tried
to convince the Purple PaintBears to meet Gregory Green, but no one
wanted to.

Suddenly, another idea came to Pauly Purple. He decided to have a party and invite all the Purple PaintBears in the neighborhood.

It would be a welcome to the Purple neighborhood party for Gregory Green. All the Purple PaintBears agreed to come even though they were nervous about meeting this Green PaintBear.

The next day, with the help of Pauly Purple's homemade chocolate chip cookies, everyone in the neighborhood came to meet Gregory Green. During the party, they learned how much they all had in common.

As everyone was having a great time, all the Purple PaintBears learned they should not have believed the rumors about Green PaintBears.

By the end of the party, all the Purple and Green PaintBears also learned it is not the color of their fur that matters but the goodness and kindness in their hearts! At that moment, all the PaintBears around the world realized God just painted them in different colors!

Quotes from the *Holy Bible* on friendship and love!

1. Whoever walks with the wise becomes wise, whoever mixes with fools will be ruined (*Proverbs 13:20*). The upright shows the way, to a friend, the way of the wicked, leads them astray (*Proverbs 12:26*).

2. Treat others, as you would like people to treat you (*Luke 6:31*). So always treat others as you would like them to treat you; that is the Law and the Prophets (*Matthew 7:12*).

3. Master, which is the great commandment in the Law? Jesus said to him, "You must love the Lord your God with all your heart, with all your soul, and with all your mind. This is the greatest and the first commandment. The second resembles it: You must love your neighbor as yourself. On these two commandments hang the whole Law, and the Prophets too" (*Matthew 22:36–40*).

About the Author

"People inspired by the Holy Spirit along
with PaintBears® and Tim Kasun"

Our Mission is to bring the
Word of God to all children throughout the world by
creating stories of truth, humility, forgiveness,
and unity which demonstrates
God's Love for Everyone of Us!

God Bless Everyone of Us!

www.paintbears.com